FEEL THE WIND

CHANDRIKA MOORTHI

ISBN 979-888521648-7

Contents

Contents

Contents

Contents

About The Co-Author

Preface

Hardness and success are like a chocolate and vanilla. Both flavours are essential to make a delicious cake. As, it is important to feel the hardness and success to realise the real fruitiness of having this life. "Feel the Wind", it expressing the life's both sides and cherish you with our words.

After every storm there will be the deadliest silent which makes us too panic of living. As, after having any kind of problems, we will be standing alone to expect the help from anyone, but there will be no one. Again, in our life we will start to crawl, but this time we determined not to walk but to fly.

Once we decide to fly, we should not look down, if we look down, even we may not afraid to fell, but the people who are all not worthy to speak of us.

Hardness is when you realise you are being isolated. But when you are isolated, you will be determined to become a success.

Everywhere is hard, when you think if surviving here is hard. So take it as fun, enjoy the essence of love, accept the hardnees and softness of life, and feel the wind....

Acknowledgements

I wholeheartedly being thankful to God, who made my first book possible.

About The Compiler

This is M. Chandrika, "Let Your Silence Speaks", this is the basic line of her life. She never speaks but her writings speak. Basically, she is an introvert but extrovert to pen and paper. She always wants to fly over the clouds. She just started her career as writer, she likes to express her views on women empowerment. She published her writings more than 25 anthologies. This is her first compiling book.

ONE

BE THE WHAT YOU WANT TO BE....

Be a butterfly in the amidst of orchard,
Not to taste honey, but to lie on the soft petals.
Be a shark in the deep ocean,
Not to show the power, but the unity.
Be the sun in the crowd,
Not to rule but to shine.
Be the moon in midst of star,
Not to be the waning moon but to be glittered.
Every person in the world, admires you,
When you attained success, but never see your wounds.
Never hides them, show them to the world,
And let your wounds be the inspiration.

-Chandrika Moorthi-

TWO

I CAN DO SOMETHING FOR MY INDIA

In the future, I want to do something for India the very first thing was that girls were safe in rape-free countries. if any rape happens boys should be killed in just one hour not many years bcz girls' safety is in our hands so boys are afraid to rape again.

second thing was that trees live we live trees cut we die If someone cuts trees the government should take very strict actions on them but we need to survive but we all trees we die to e trees to save ourselves.♥?

small kids under 14 work they don't have money to study they don't have a house to live in they don't have food to eat, they don't have clothes to wear in India? soo in the future government should take actions regarding their small kids so they also do something for their future ♥?

say no to child marriage small girls and boys their parents get pressure to do marriage their kids under the age of 18 it's not right thing, if you can not take care of your child then pls don't bear them if you do that your kid's lives will be wasted.

Don't hit animals, animals are so sweet you hit them you ree so cruel so in future, if any person hits animals there is very strict punching on them bcz animals are better than humans.

in the future, I do something that provides free food, books fewer school less fees, to those children who don't have money to study.

Alot of things I really want to do in my future for my country

-Aanya-

About The Co-Author

-Aanya-

I am aanya I m writer..I m in 12 classs...I m co author of many books I love to write wht I feel no matter what people think about me... I want to change my this hobbie into my passion...I m numelogiest nd taro card reader also. I m 17 years old nd I believe in karma.

THREE

FEEL THE WIND

A boatman sings and sails in his raft
Wishing some good times to come
My people sends me off building
hope
Now I am far and more from my little hut's
door
And reached the sea with deadly roar.

Slowly the shore out of my sight
The waves that took me to the terrific
height
I am the only soul who is sole
In this bluish whole to play a fisherman's
role
With hope to catch atleast a shoal
To fill my people's empty bowl.

The song of a boatman
Might not be so sweet to greet
But it's my only mate
To cross this eternal fate

FEEL THE WIND

The sun bids me goodbye
The stars that twinkles joy
I continued my way in search of prey

What happens if the furious sea
wants to take me with her
My boat will be drunk
And I surely will sink
Will the god bring
Someone to save me with a wing
I gonna blink and think
Just blink and think.....

Just then my stupid mind realises
That it was a lucid dream
I believe my heart is fearlessly firm
Then why should I grim?
The two extremes, the sky and the sea
Though very distant meets in an instant
Such miracles can be seen
When you look at the neverending sea.

Cross your boundary line
Everything will be definitely fine
Start to train your brain
To drain the strain that keeps you plain

You can feel the wind
That never ever end

Which helps you as a friend
The wind of happiness
That blows forever
And showers you with flower.

-Abinaya Selvakumar-

FOUR

TO THE NATURE

Dear lovable nature,

Hii dear. It's been long seeing you happy. How are you now? I know it's not so good to ask you such question. Even I am not good. I am hardly living with my heavy heart and unbearable guilt. This is a letter to you. I know that now you are so busy in various states and countries all over the world giving people in return for our merciless presents that we have given you for years. But take a break and see to my letter. It's my friendly request.

Let us go back to our past, the happy past. We both were beautiful with smiling face, healthy and glowing looks. We played together, you showered me rain to make me wet. You flings me breeze and I stand in freeze. I could remember everything but can't find the one thing that make us depart. Am I the reason? Sometimes I think of it and fed in guilt. I miss you a lot and you have now started to teach me the lesson for my known mistakes. I felt really bad for what I have done and butter you to the extremity. How long will you tolerate even if I am your friend. I salute to your patience.

We both stand in the opposite ends in every aspect. You love me but I hurt you to the core. You helped me but in return I killed you. A single sorry will not be enough for the blunder I did. But it's already late to realise, so that I have decided to ask you a chance to prove myself good to you as you are to me.

Though the children keep on doing mistakes the mom never stops loving her children. She can't hate her own kids though they are bad. So, pardon me and take me as a child on your hands and let us start our new life with equal love and happiness. Slowly everything will recover, don't worry.

From the lover of nature.

-Abinaya Selvakumar-

About The Co-Author

Abinaya Selvakumar

Abinaya Selvakumar, pursuing her BA degree has an extreme passion towards writing still her childhood. She loves to explore her thoughts through poetry. This poetry on feel the wind is also a small try to mirror herself with her words expecting love and support. She is also a budding writer in kahaniya.

FIVE

THOSE DAYS OF STRUGGLES

Now when I remember those days of flood, I had gone through the toughest days of my life for the first time. At first I enjoyed the water coming without knowing the horrible effects afterwards. I made paper boats with my kids and splashes through the water. I took videos and pictures of those beautiful nature. But later I could realise the real face of mother nature who has both the power of creation and destruction. Suddenly the environment changed to dark. The cold wind was blowing. We were hurrying packing our baggages . We were forced to move to another house. Later on we changed two more houses due to the flood. We were watching the river with the worst condition. The colour of the water changed to muddy colour. Those horrible moments made me realise the truth that in front of nature man is nothing. If we do good to nature,she will protect us .

-Anu Filda Varghese-

SIX

THE PHOENIX BIRD IN ME

I am the Phoneix within me
Burned in the words and mocking
Of the people around me
But I persisted upon my
strength and believes
I come back with my
Whole energy and will power
Which always within me
From the words that prick me
I will come up one day
As a Phoneix bird...

-Anu Filda Varghese-

About The Co-Author

Ms.Anu Filda Varghese

Ms.Anu Filda Varghese is currently working as an Assistant Professor on Contract at Carmel College Mala. She has published many articles in different journals of repute. She has presented many papers in both national and International conferences. She has four years of experience in teaching.

SEVEN

RAZIA AND SULTANA

Story of women in contemporary India facing hypocrisy in the institution of marriage. How should a wife deal with it? Family, friends, colleagues can only offer so much support and redressal, legal approach is traumatic to say the least. So, should a woman take the law into her hands?

-Dr. Fahmeeda.P-

EIGHT

LEARNING TO SPEAK TO FATHER

LEARNING TO SPEAK TO FATHER

I enter the house, the dewan cot, the sofa, the plastic chairs, the landline telephone instrument are all in their familiar places in the hall. The centre table has the day's newspaper unopened, unread folded neatly. Nothing has changed; the familiar position of the furniture gives some comfort. The television screen on the wall blinks with different images, colourful, vibrant, loud and incessant. The clock on the wall says seven and quite furtively, on auto mode I check my wristwatch. Waiting for my father to come into the hall, I give the showcase on the wall a thorough look.

I notice a number of attractions in the showcase, from the travels of my parents – reminders of the happy time. They are from holy places, from Paris, Rome, Switzerland, Disneyland and the like. A miniature Chinese man carrying a rather long staff on his left shoulder a cloth bundle on one end and a pearl hanging from the other end, a miniature decorative ladies shoe hanging askew from the miniature Eifel tower of Paris, and a camel permanently trotting with a young Arab boy on its back, jostle for space. The contents in the immediate section below bring home life's inevitable reality of ill health and disease in the form of different sized plastic boxes full of tablets, capsules, tonics, powders and oils from different branches of medicine. This section which promises cures occupies a central position now going by its rather pell-mell status, while the other contents of the showcase are in their exact places and appear forlorn, covered in a fine layer of dust. It appears as if the person who was interested in maintaining them has lost interest now.

As my eyes move to the clock on the wall yet again, my father enters the hall slowly, advancing step by step tentatively taking his time and sits on the sofa. The first words he utters are the routine "How are you?" in a feeble voice. It's a shock to listen to him these days, his voice a far cry from the robust, active and jovial self of the past. I make the usual noises about the wellbeing of myself and my family members. The conversation which had barely begun comes to a stop. After a pause it is now my turn to ask him the same question, to which he replies in the positive, his health is fine. Again there is a pause, a longer one this time as I ask, if he finished his dinner. He replies affirmatively yet again. My mind begins to think of questions to ask him, things to say, topics to discuss, share my thoughts but something holds me back. I think of saying this asking that, but I only keep thinking, because I know he'll only agree with me, he doesn't want to talk and discuss. I get the feeling he wants to be left alone.

My younger brother seated on the other sofa speaks loudly almost shouting, "Abba, Didi has come, speak to her". Slowly my father nods his head. I look at him now, shocked by his physical *appearance – he has had a haircut, his usual healthy crop of salt and pepper hair trimmed rather short for the summer, he is dressed in half sleeved white vest and knee length shorts. His face has scratch marks and looks shriveled; his eyes appear beady, empty, emotionless, his limbs full of red ugly rashes due to disease, and his body emaciated and scrawny.*

As I look at his hands now afflicted with allergy, out of blue I recall an incident from my college days. I had been elected president of the college union and on the night of the valedictory event he had come to take me back home due to the late hour. Riding pillion I had fallen off my father's TVS moped due to sheer exhaustion. Thankfully the speed had been too slow to cause loss of limb or life, but I remember how my father had held my chafed and inflamed right hand in his hands and expressed dismay that I would have trouble writing my exams. He had taken care of the bruises not just with medical attention but encouraged me to practice writing slowly at home so that the pain would not be more when I answered the question paper at a stretch for three hours. I look at his rash ridden hands helplessly unable to do anything to relieve him of the pain.

It is difficult to converse with my father. He suffered brain stroke and fell in the bathroom two years ago. The doctors predict a steady deterioration of the mind and the body. Strangely he doesn't express words missing his wife as his mind has gone back to his childhood, for he recalls his siblings, his youngest sister who now lives abroad and wants to stay with her. He recalls the distant past quite clearly and scolds his irresponsible brother-in-law, the youngest sister's husband for deserting her, after having two children. "Bewaqoof aadmi! No concern for his wife and kids, running off to live in a monastery like that, the rascal" without any power to match the words...just empty words, recalling the past hurt emotions. My brother and I are surprised at this sudden outburst as it has been a long time of more than thirty years since this event in the family. Not once does he ask for his wife whom he unusually used to address as Kya, no aji sunte ho, or biwi, or begum. Seldom have I heard my parents address each other by name, for my mother would tell one of her children to "call Abba".

I realize I have to learn to speak to my father now in the permanent absence of my mother for she had taken on the role of the speaker of my father's words and even thoughts. In the previous visits when I asked my father about his health, it was always my mother who gave detailed accounts of what he had eaten, which medicine he had been prescribed and even what my father had replied to the doctor's questions. Now with my mother's passing away the via-media is lost forever...

When my eyes move from my father and come to rest on the dewan, my heart skips a beat and tears come unbidden to my eyes. With an effort I control them, not willing to let my father see my tears and go through the pain of separation from his spouse of fifty years afresh.

In the past, whenever I came to my mother's house in the evenings, I would find her relaxing on the dewan with either the remote of the television or the newspaper in her hands, after the evening walk in the neighbouring park. If a serial on television interested her she would watch it otherwise read the newspaper or a magazine. An avid reader, a stickler to keeping schedules and a wonderful home maker, she would perform her daily activities according to a time table drawn by her. Now that place on the dewan cot is empty for its owner has left for the heavenly abode leaving her children and spouse devastated.

My father is forlorn and we the siblings heartbroken and despondent.

The landline rings, it is a courtesy call from one of my mother's friends from the laughter club. Suddenly I recall the happy evening I had spent not so long ago, when we had an animated conversation regarding the activities of her laughter club. My mother had participated in a word puzzle game and won the first place. This narration had led to recalling a similar event by my aged father from his college days. He had won a prize for his mathematical ability in a competition. There had been no dearth of words then, conversation had been effortless, how quickly time had flown, and my brother and I had looked on happily taking a backseat as my father and mother spoke of past and the present. I had not looked at the clock at all then, whereas my eyes now move towards it constantly.
Now there is silence due to the absence of the person who knit the web of love, affection and care towards each other. Her absence speaks louder than words. My heart cries, where is she? When would we see her? My heart cries for the din in my ears due to the silence in the hall is unbearable and forever.

-Dr. Fahmeeda.P-

About The Co-Author

Dr. Fahmeeda. P

works as Assistant Professor in English. For her teaching is a passion from childhood and writing is a necessary art. She looks at people objectively as characters for her writing and analyses issues of society. She loves to read and the contemporary writers are her favourites.

NINE

MEND MY MIND

An appeal to The God to mend my crooked mind and refine
me as a son of Him.
Asking God to mend my mind

About The Co-Author

-Dr. V. Suresh-

Dr. V. Suresh, Head, Department of English, Government Arts and Science College Gudalur has a strong passion for creative writing and resource person in creative writing.

TEN

THE JOY OF CHILDHOOD FRIENDSHIP

My Heart is the comfy place
which is embedded with rejuvenating reminiscences.
My feelings for you are but a variegated kaleidoscopic
Spectrum
which diffuses diversified sentiments.

My heart cherishes distant-bound memories.
No absolute necessity to pour my heart out.
The very thought about you
instigates instant smile on my face.

My heart being a reservoir of emotions,
Never overflows or gets decrepit;
No scientist can ever gauge
how much amiability my little heart can accommodate.

-Dr. V. Anuradha-

ELEVEN
MY FLUFFY CAT

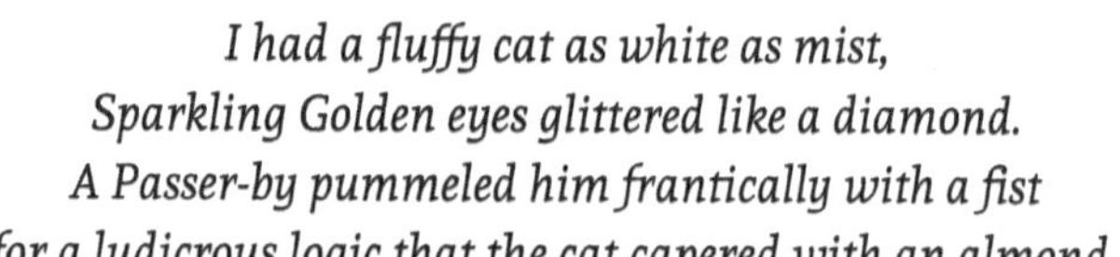

I had a fluffy cat as white as mist,
Sparkling Golden eyes glittered like a diamond.
A Passer-by pummeled him frantically with a fist
for a ludicrous logic that the cat capered with an almond.

My mother brought him home where he sniffed around,
His musical voice scratches at the footsteps of outsiders;
Sudden showering of the coziness and pleasure by the arrival of
this little friend.
My house has been transformed into an ethereal abode of bliss.

A jubilant ball of feathery fur
Resting on my lap with a musical murmur.
Folding his claws, a symbol of birr.
After a colossal yawn, he took a long winter slumber.

-Dr. V. Anuradha-

TWELVE

AN ANECDOTE ON MY EXPERIENCE IN A PHOTO STUDIO

Ten years ago, I went to a studio along with my husband for the purpose of taking a passport size photo. The manager asked me to await a while. I waited there for almost half an hour. Then he directed me to a room. The photographer was a teenage girl. She was grave and glanced at me without zeal. I witnessed that girl walking from that room to the reception umpteen number of times that too at a snail's pace which ultimately revealed her disinterested attitude. She asked me to be seated. While I slightly inquired her, she responded that she had got to dash off immediately. I came to know that her co-worker who must have been there by that time had not yet turned up. All of a sudden, a girl entered as fast as the streaming rain. The Photographer started scolding that girl for her belated arrival. It must have been a sudden rush of blood to the head that prompted them

to have such an unceasing argument. The photographer started enlisting a series of instructions without even looking at my face. I followed her advice blindly. She instructed to me, "Don't turn your head. Turn your face". A sea of agitated thoughts and frustrated feelings engulfed my mind on hearing that statement. It was quite natural that I desired to get my photo in a satisfactory condition. So I did not lose my temper. In the words of George Meredith, I was 'as obedient as a puppet'. I heard the 'click' sound within an eye wink which made me realize that the photo was taken. I left the room and went to the manager's desk. In a fit of fury, I asked him "How is it possible for anyone to turn his or her countenance without shaking head?" We left the place before he tried to pacify me. When I recounted that incident to the members of my family, everyone burst into laughter. I could not help but recall the adage 'One man's trash is another man's treasure'. The whole week before I got back my photo, I was as restless as a cat on hot bricks because I had assumed that I might perhaps have to face the similar bitter experience as confronted by Stephen Leacock, the reputed English writer. Contradictory to my pre-conceived notion, I received my photo as an exact replica of my visage. Literally, my joy knew no bounds.

-Dr. V. Anuradha-

THIRTEEN

THE BOOK THAT TRANSFORMED MY LIFE

The book which has tremendously captivated my vision and mission is Paulo Coelho's The Alchemist, an international book seller with over 65 million copies sold worldwide and translated in about 56 languages. This novel, which I received as an accolade from Reader's Digest in the year 2001, has abundantly guided me to acquire the indispensable skills one needs to strive to thrive in life. This decipherable book is a magical story of an Andalusian young Shepherd named Santiago and his pursuit of mundane riches at the Egyptian Pyramids after having a reiterated motif assisted me to have an ingrained implication upon my life. The whole journey has taught me to grasp the essentiality to follow my instincts and dreams. As Dr. A.P.J. Abdul Kalam has promptly pointed out the significance of transforming our dreams into profound thoughts which in turn will lead to germane action, Paulo Coelho has also emphasized that the possibility of having a dream come true makes life alluring. Moreover, the line 'The Secret of life is to fall seven

times and to get up eight times' has provoked me to study diligently and get through State Level Eligibility Test and also to overcome umpteen number of crucial hurdles in my life. In addition to this, the lines from this explicable book, "Don't give in to your fears. If you do, you won't be able to talk to your heart" gave room for the realization of how I should be bold and motivated me to make my dreams get accomplished without being inflicted by the fear of failure. Moreover I have also ascertained that we should not hesitate to seize the opportunity at the right moment. This cognition is well evident from the line "When you want something, all the universe conspires in helping you to achieve it". As the adage goes "Books break the shackles of time, my joy knows no bounds whenever I happen to fix my eyes upon this book.

-Dr. V. Anuradha-

FOURTEEN

My Drowning Experience in the Sea

A visit to Poompuhar during the summer vacation when I completed Standard VIII had stamped a deeper impact as an unforgettable incident in my life. Due to exalted curiosity, I felt very much hesitant to obey my mother's words despite her persistent plea and cautionary mandate. I was obstinate that I wished to enjoy more due to the first time visit to the seashore and I was reluctantly unwilling to clasp my mother's hands. In spite of my mother's repetitive warnings, suddenly I got vanished out of everyone's sight as though of a magical spell. Everything happened within an eye wink and the joyous scene was shifted to that full of desperation. Everyone of us tried out their best so as to locate my presence. At that juncture, one of my relatives pinpointed to my mother, "Sister! See, a big blue coloured ball is floating on the water". My mother got very much stunned as the ball that he had pointed to her happened to me who was wearing a blue-coloured umbrella frock stitched by my mother. She instantly started to get into the sea water

so as to search my whereabouts. The crowd warned my mother to give up that Herculean task as I had been carried away by the sea waves to a long distance. My mother did not drop her deed. On the contrary, she started lumbering over the waves and after reaching a particular distance, she could see my hair that too only during the ebb and flow of sea waves. She approached further and tactfully clasped the clutches of my hair and dragged me out with the utmost strength and brought me safely to the shore. She then made me collect few pebbles from the shore so as to recover me from the mental shock. The audacious attempt of my mother is still being praised by everyone.

-Dr. V. Anuradha-

About The Co-Author

-Dr. V. Anuradha-

Dr. V. Anuradha M.A(Eng)., M.Phil., M.A(Ling)., SET., Ph.D has eight years of teaching experience. At present, she is working as Assistant Professor in the Department of English in Vellalar College for Women, Erode, Tamilnadu, India. She is interested in Freelance Writing and Translation. She has published around 5 research papers in National and International Journals and Conferences. Her Research area comprises Indian writing in English and English Language Teaching.

FIFTEEN
My Identity

When Hyma was twenty one years old, her life's new door opened.

She asked herself "Is this the life of a married woman?'".Hyma was an educated,enthusiastic and energetic girl.After her marriage she transformed herself into a new woman. She chocked herself in the four walls of the room. She could not endure her circumstances. She felt "My torments will not end within a day, a month and an year. She asked herself"What is my role? "What is my identity?"
Her sense of Identity and determination prompted her to raise as a Phoenix.She jumped out of the door and commenced a new way of delight and exploration.

-Hima Harry-

SIXTEEN
RED MASKS

Riya and Priya were cousins. They lived together in a flat near the town.

One day, Riya was too late to reach the flat. Priya dialed her many times.

But she could not connect her. Suddenly, she heard an unexpected sound

in the kitchen . Her heart seemed to be broken. Finally, she moved to the kitchen

with shivering hands. When she saw two black dressed men in the kitchen,

she collapsed. On the next morning, she woke up in a strange room with Riya.

The black dressed men were sitting near them. Riya asked."Who are you?

"Why are you kidnapped us?." The two men offered two boxes to them and forced them to

open the boxes. When they opened, they saw two red beautiful masks in the boxes.

They saw some words are imprinted on "Wear the mask" "Save Your life".These men

revealed their identity and expressed their true love towards

them . It was on February,14th.
The girls became very happy and they wore the Red masks.

-Hima Harry-

SEVENTEEN
My Clouds

When I looked at myself
I could not perceive anything
I could not receive anything
I search for;
my identity
I became powerless
Clouds of cowardice;
revolved around me.

-Hima Harry-

About The Co-Author

Ms.Hima Harry

Ms.Hima Harry is working as an Assistant Professor on Contract at
Carmel College, Mala. Her poems have been published in many anthologies like "One Hundred Shades of Love", The Ether Euphony", "Love River" , "Flying Poetics" and" Creative Flight Journal". She has presented many research papers in National and
International Conferences. She has published articles and book chapters in International Journals and Books. She has received World Book of Record, Asian Book of Record and Indian Book of Record.

EIGHTEEN

FEEL THE WIND

To my blood member Pavithran,

I think this is my first letter that am writing to u as a sibling in the past 2 decades.I know we are not brought up with an ethic which others follows.Totally we two are from other side of ethic life.From our younger age of below 5 we two are being negotiated from everything which is the basic need of the child at that age.The two souls of our grand parents hold our hands to move ahead in our life with the garden of positivity.But after their loss I think we are under crisis till now of being aching for that warmth of love and care.We were like a broken glasses of not being able to fix our feelings at any stage.Thats the place where I thought we are alone in this whole globe.We started to face our problems and worries by themselves at our beginning of the life .This made us softhearted person as individual of two of us.We started to place our flaws into victory but the super power around us made us to live in only the pain.The suffer of being alone and instead of sharing our feelings with others ,we handled our own problems by not saying to anyone at any cost with a blower heart.This made us to bare all fails and sorrows in and around us.But we stood up to be atleast survive in this globe.As long as we grow,the length of the pains is being increasing till date.But no worries am not the one sister who opens with u often.I know am not the one who is perfect at anything but am free to feel others by standing on their shoes.I too have flaws and I too do mistakes.But you are also trying hard to fit me strong and am along with you in that process.I know u work hard to make our life happy.The kin and kith may throw the arrow on us by seeing our own decisions and own life.Whatever the others says or do it to u.Whoever might blame us and fight with us and forces u to be not by urself and the one who pulls our leg at our environment ,keep it mind at one day we gonna make our flaws into victory of being in our own kingdom.Whenever u feel stressed regarding family or office work or in a relationship or among the society , please just TAKE A LONG BREATHE AND FEEL THE WIND WHICH BLOWS ON U.Because u the super power of ur own.Not others view or opinion or their suggestions will make u move longer in life.Its just only u.Whatever the extinct is ,the decision and effort that u done by analysing it by urself with full efforts will make u succeed one day for sure.Lets make these puddles into a new step of new life.I promise you that i will be holding ur hands at every situation in our boon life .Till that bare me at every flaws and mistakes.I know I hurted you many times at many stages but I sware that ,thats not my pair of words in the view of hurting or blaming you.It happened in a way of unknowingly ,So sorry for the pain that I am giving u till now.Hope to be recognised soon in our life.Stay strong my boy.Let the changes will hit us hard soon.Proud to be sharing the same blood with u.RATHER THAN FEELING DOWN,STAY STRONG WITH HOPE .Let's colour our life beautiful with only happiness and joy and loads of satisfactions. Love u tonnes with a drop of venom.

- with loads of love,
ur sister,
Janani

- Janani chandrasekaran-

NINETEEN
BE YOURSELF

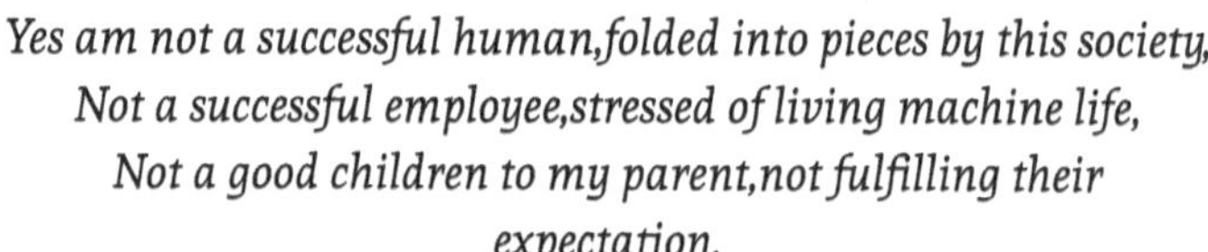

Yes am not a successful human,folded into pieces by this society,
Not a successful employee,stressed of living machine life,
Not a good children to my parent,not fulfilling their
expectation,
Not a good student,by grabbing the teacher's tips of success.
Not a good friend,to help them in every single situation,
Not a good human,to help the needy who is suffering more
than my inner soul,
Not a good observer, of not finding the stone which throws on
my life by my around members ,
Not a hardworker but trying not to be lazy atleast,
Not a fake one of playing with others feelings,
Not a great social activist to serve my responsibilities to the
society,
Not a lovely one to be liked by everyone,
Not a selfish one,to enough my own company at my own
kingdom,
Not a heartless one,to bare others backstabs.
Your flaws and mistakes makes u even more perfect.So Just BE
URSELF AND LOVE URSELF OF WHOM U ARE..Let your vibe
of individuality spark every where.

CHANDRIKA MOORTHI

-Janani Chandrasekaran-

About The Co-Author

Janani chandrasekaran

An young girl with plenty of dreams.Let the sky be my limit.HOPE AND BELIEVE IN PROCESS

TWENTY

DETERRED FACE: ACID ATTACK VICTIM

The day was pleasant, birds peeps around,
The dead leaves and plastic bags rolled round.
The heavy wind splashed on my face,
Nature moved in a spiral like our personal lives.

Suddenly, I, heard a voice calling my name,
Before I could react, something slapped me.
I, felt like liter of candle wax was gashed on my face,
And some four to five butcher knives were tearing me into
pieces.

I, crawled and rolled on road,
While the acid derived my skin on the road.
I, cried and screamed,
I heard a few shout and yell calling for help.

When I gained conscious and opened my eyes,

FEEL THE WIND

I found that my dreams were shattered into pieces.
Because I saw only my eyes were open,
Part of my ears, nose, chin and cheek were eaten.

When I returned home all pitied me,
But no one was ready to support me.
They neglected me for my appearance,
But I neglected them for their insanity.

He throw acid on me to burn up my beauties,
YOU there, it's my body that's dead but still my soul breathes.

- Ms. Jeevitha L,

About The Co-Author

Mrs. Jeevitha L

Mrs. Jeevitha L has 6 years of teaching experience and has obtained her M. Phil. in Indian Writing in English from Bharathiar University, Coimbatore, Tamil Nadu and pursing her Ph. D. from Bharathiar University, Coimbatore, Tamil Nadu. She also adds to her credit, certificate courses on Soft Skill Developments, Writing for Media and Writing Tools and Hacks: Copy Writing/ Blogging/ Content Writing and is certified with BEC Vantage certificate from Cambridge University. She has published 11 papers in UGC approved journal with ISSN numbers and 3 papers with ISBN Number.

TWENTY-ONE
A Sparrow's Life

•❦•

A Sparrow's Life
The world is waiting for the sunrise, the sun slowly comes out of the sky and during that time, the sounds 'chirup' and 'cheeps' can be heard. A huge tree is here provides shadow and shelter for many. From that tree the beautiful sounds can be heard. On a branch of the tree a little sparrow and it's family is living. They collect small broken tree branches and build a beautiful house and live happily.The tree and it's surrounding looks beautiful, just like a forest .The sparrows spent time there in the evening and lived ever so happily..

One day a loud sound was heard. The sparrows and their families came out of their nest. They don't know what was happening around, and saw a huge vehicle slowly cutting the tree. Their beautiful house was about to fall, The eggs which were ready for hatching start to fall . With hopeless feelings the sparrows start flying here and there. Within few hours the tree was cut down. A more than two decades old tree, was no more now.

The sparrows started to fly elsewhere to build their nest. They might find a tree to build their nest but they might not feel the same happiness like they did here.
When their nest get broken the sparrow flying hopelessly, likewise me and my family run here and there when they start destroying our beautiful house.
With lots of tears in my eyes and a dried tone I cry. Like the sparrows we too start to migrate to some other place.
We won't be able to fight against them, because no one will listen to the words of a stupid common man.

Soon after the construction work was started and a huge bridge was built.
A year later i visited that place, now lot of vehicles going over the bridge. Then i noticed that None of the shopping malls, star rated hotels, apartments were damaged during the construction of the bridge...
Whenever there is a welfare scheme, people like us starts suffer.

-Kannan Mohan-

About The Co-Author

Kannan Mohanraj

I'm Kannan Mohanraj. Agriculture Engineering graduate and current working in Irrigation company. I tries to write the story of people who has nothing left in their life other than hardwork and slavery. And my dream is to be a film maker.
My Instagram id - mohanrajkannan
My mail id - kannanmahi77@gmail.com

TWENTY-TWO
ECSTASY OF TRAVEL

Ecstasy of travel

Once you start enjoying the feeling of moving on, nothing can bring you down other than your own attachment.

few decades back traveling around is hard because of the transportation and the dangers that arrive in the path although a lot of people choose to travel in search of better livelihood and a form of escaping from their boredom.among those few of them choose to move constantly and never settled down despite of their financial situations and hardships they face because of inconsistency. how bad the situation got with a smile on their face they faced more fears than anyone at their comfortable turfs. they were in touch of their souls longing and dedicated themselves to fulfill it.

" language of universe is incapable of teaching but learned by thyself"

our millennial generation are found lost around concrete jungles and go through the worst and at a point they start wondering 'what the hell is happening to me?' and eventually start punishing themselves with toxic thoughts. same as our ancestors we too travel whenever we can and more frequently than them we move around because of our transportation development. We choose to move only when it's necessary and even plan the travel with every inch of detail. It lowers our spirits and we are caught up in the planning.

If The people who are caught up at a day to day job Try to break their routine and they will find their life meaningless, nothing intimates them. We can't deny the fact that it's the century we live in. The amount of shit we took at work causes worry and stress but it's the only thing that induces the hormones of pleasure. In case a wealthier goes through the same discomfort they look for the connection they can make in Order to outgrow themselves and build up Their business to a whole new level. Understanding that Whoever the person may be, they too handle the same discomforts you handle but at different levels. Is that our purpose really? To work for your daily expenses and exhausted both the way. What's going to cure those defects it causes? Why?

Unexpectedly the answer to that is simple rest and recharging your spirit becomes tough nowadays. It leads us to our ancestors' way of exploring the unknown by feeling the wise words of the breeze that goes through your hair around your ear, whispering beauty trying to expose us to the secrets of everything. The places we move have the tendency to act as a doctor, healer, advisor etc.. which place are you in now? Nothing can refill the emptiness you face than NATURE. Those endless waves at the sea makes wonder Their dance moves with a melody they cause through The movements. Even if you are left alone in a forest you can never feel lonely because of the surrounding environment. Those reptiles and mammals are not going to let you experience the feeling, insects living under the fallen leaves creates an ecosystem of Their own. Realising the presence of our mother earth is a pure bliss. At those moments Without even considering your spirit gets healthier by drawing the energy directly from the source of creation itself. You Will witness the fading anxiety, depression and make your heart feel lighter than a hair from a feather.

For Our generation it is easier to access the bad influences than good ones. As commoners we travel more than a thousand kilometres a year and yet with no time to Lift ourselves up because of the influences. Enjoyment comes from external stimulants but when it wears off the condition surely will get worse than before.

You may get the question: will it ease your worries? . Yes! Absolutely it will.

"Feel the tides turning your way and
rise above! "

-Karthigai selvan M-

About The Co-Author

Karthigai selvan M

Karthi is a common man in search of abyss.

TWENTY-THREE
MARRY ME

MARRY ME,

"I'm fine " Is the favorite phrase of priya. If you are an Indian you will probably hear that name at least 1 lakh times before you die because it is a typical house hold name in India.she is someone with whom your parents would allow you to play with because she never causes any trouble. If there is a Nobel Prize for a good girl then she would at least get nominated from India. But wait,let's start our time time machine and look what she looks like when she is 30.Based on the list of qualities we have seen above you would probably think she is either got married as her parents wished or became a doctor to serve the society . But hold your horses ... She is neither married nor a doctor. She is still single at the age of 30 , when you are an Indian woman that's when your neighborhood children consider you as an aunty. And also she has a daughter whom she adopted from an orphanage. This is a violation of all the traditional norms and values of the people around her. But why did she choose to do so?. I was curious too .When I asked her about her drastic change She told me that she found her sense of self lost while trying to fit in with her family, relatives and every single *person around her.she stopped doing things that would please others and stared doing things which matters to her and her only. That's when she came to be known as a rebel , a whore etc.. around the same neighborhood. The last words she said still echoes in my head, she said "stop waiting for someone to ask you ' will you marry me' instead ask yourself 'WILL YOU MARRY ME for better,for worse, in sickness and in health, untill death do us apart".That's when I asked myself " WILL YOU MARRY ME " and she said "I will" . And we have been happily married for years and will be for years to come. What about you stranger? Have you got married to the beautiful person on the earth yet? If you haven't it's never too late...*

-Kavipriya-

TWENTY-FOUR

I WONDER

What if I am no longer that girl who used to be obedient?
I Wonder if it would hurt the reputation that I've been maintaining.. Maybe
What if I stop trying my best in education when they say all I'm going to be, all I'm ever going to be is
A wife to a man, a mother to a son
Nothing more
Nothing less...
I Wonder if I should keep believing their words..

Then what should I do about the stories of Kalpana chawla and Mother Teresa, Sania Mirza who fed my dreams and hopes..
I wonder whether they heard the same words from the society..
I Wonder whether I would be able to create an identity as a woman rather than being identified as a certain person's wife..
I wonder how many girls are made to believe that the purpose of her degree is,for her to get married to an educated man
Rather than her wish to become a scientist

I wonder if I ever question them would they call me a feminist or

Would it make them say "that's why we should have never given her education in the first place"
I WONDER..

-Kavipriya-

About The Co-Author

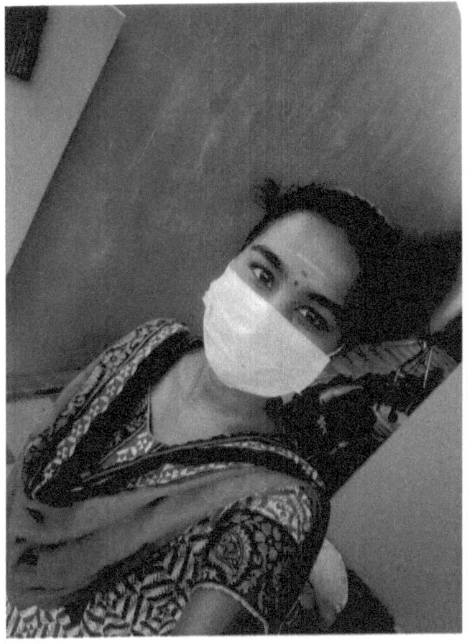

Kavipriya

Kavi priya is a soul who wishes to inspire others by her writing. She is a newbie in the writing world..

TWENTY-FIVE

LIFE CHANGER OF A GIRL

In a village called Kaikolmedu Sunitha and her family lived a very simple life but she was not happy. She is interested in many fields like Archaeology, dance, painting, and more. She could not try those areas because her family is not rich instead they are a simple middle class family. Her name was Supriya, her main motive was to take care of her family. Some of the incidents strongly stored in her mind that her mother told that she was worried for a female child taking care of the family and her father also worried he would lose job because of a female child born to them. Supriya had a younger sister and she would like to live as a strong child to protect family. These are the situations of Supriya and her family. Supriya wanted to earn money so she developed her skills and tried doing online jobs without the knowledge of her family members because she had a fear of what would happen if her parents stopped her in an online job. Her sister Anushya was a good sister who helped her sister Supriya to cross every hurdle.

Their parents were strict enough to control both their children from the thought of achievements. They wanted their children to be with them and helpful and no need to achieve anything and not needed to make them popular. Supriya's words are always not accepted by her parents. She should follow the way they showed to her and only their decisions were accepted by Supriya. Sometimes she suffered in stress but moved her mind to get relaxed mostly.

One day she got to know about Researcher Balu, who was 58 years old and she attended his speech under the topic Kumari kandam. There he shared about his whats app group and his contact number. She joined that within two days after attending an interview for joining that group and she passed in that. She got to know about him that he is a master in seventy two fields. She got more knowledge in that daily more details shared in that group one day a group member shared information on mind exercises and meditation. Supriya was interested to learn that more and she bought some books and read about that. She found the power of her mind, she would know what will happen in future whether good or bad she would aware herself.

Likewise oneday night she had a dream that a lady came and said,"do not lose Balu he is your life changer, will guide you to achieve". Supriya understood that her life will change through his guidance. The next day Balu sent his parents's photo to show how his parents achieved in those days. Supriya supposed to see that picture and said to Balu about the dream she had last night and the lady who came was Balu's mother. He said, "you are lucky my mother would not come in dream even in my dream only twice to aware me that's it other than not came still". Supriya was happy and speaking about some group messages.

The next day a poem competition was conducted in that "Youngsters" group. Supriya participated in that and won first prize. She also learnt to write more standard form by Balu. Her mind questioned to her that how come an researcher able to help and develop every single persons in that group. She was eager to know about his adventurous life history, she asked him about it and he also started to share, he said, "from my age of twenty five I was researching about the hidden place Kumari Kandam. My research was getting successful through the sea route of Turtles. Turtles were the route for countries to sale or purchase goods in ancient days, so this method I used for my research and once I brought Turtle to home for research my parents scolded me badly, my father started to beat, they said Turtle is a negative omen and also I was not allowed inside the home for many days. At that time I was feared not for my research but for my lady love, I loved a girl who supported me for my growth. I tried to make my parents to accept her but they planned to kill her. So, we both escaped and I continued my research.

Only at my age of fifty two i was succeeded, populared, got supports from others, but my parents not here with me both passed away a few years ago now this group I created for developing talented kids". After hearing this, Supriya started to work as an associater for him. After a month a list of active and talented youngsters were selected in that group to develop them more. In that list Supriya's name was there and she promoted as one of the members in management team of that group. She was very happy when she tried to share this to her parents, they not listened to her words as usual. After a week, a cool morning she got to knew that she was selected for an award 'multi talented girl'. She said to her friends and said to her parents in joy. Her parents asked about her activities. Supriya was shocked and surprised that for the first time in her life they were asking about her activities and were listening to her words. She then understood that actions have the power than words. The next day at evening she had a call from Balu that he went to interview but he wanted youngsters to take interview for *brilliant questions. Supriya was thinking about taking interview but not replied anything except "Ok", "good bye". He then posted his same desire in group about interview. She then suddenly asked a chance to take interview, at that time another girl named Meenakchi in that group asked to him a day for an interview. Supriya prayed to get a chance for an interview, and by god's grace she was fixed for an interview the next week. She met her friends in library to convey this news and conveyed this happy news in a husky voice at night she given party for the first success in her life. Her friend Sudha asked, "is this interview that much important". Supriya replied yes, and this interview will be seen by more people and likewise if she tried to take more interviews and populared she had a possibility to enter into cini field.*

Her friends were overwhelmed in happy, all encouraged and enjoyed the party. After a week she woke up early and was making up for an interview. She conveyed this to her parents and her said to go along with mother. She replied "Ok" and she moved along with her mother and Supriya asked some important questions. After an interview everyone in that place praised her for such brilliant questions and also praised her mother for such brilliant daughter she have. Supriya's mother was exsastic and hugged her. She informed this happy news to everyone through mobile phone and she started believing her daughter that her daughter was a talented girl. Supriya's parents from that day onwards supported her a lot and lived a happy life. Supriya thanked god for given her a person, who is her life changer.

-M. Sobiga-

TWENTY-SIX
RIVER

River sparkle in its way;
it reflects the world, like mirror that cast my face.
Not exhausted a bit, always in motion.
Arduous to handle, but adoptable to situation.
Sometimes mixture of rainwater,
Provoke its anger in hazardous way.
The overflow of water,
is a deluge, that swallows everything.
When its anger subside,
it is a symbol of peace.
Learn from river,
It teaches to act in perfect time.

-M. Sobiga-

TWENTY-SEVEN

My Soul &
Conscience

My soul merged with a voice,
It is a silent melody, my eyes searches for that,
And my ears listen to that whispering, Ohh! this is a dirge.
My lips questioned, but why my soul cry?
May be something ruinous? my body works in confusion.
Ears heard a conversation, my conscience told soul,
You are tired of hurdles and failures.
Everyone's soul need confidence;
It gives freshness, but you cried.
Tears are mixture of salt and water,
Likewise body and soul, not vary
One affects another, must work in unison.

-M. Sobiga-

About the Co-Author

-Sobiga. M-

I am Sobiga. M, I am an B.A graduate, from Erode. Interest in writing field. Trained to write lyrics and good in Tamil poems.

TWENTY-EIGHT

YOU ARE INCREDIBLY AWESOME

*YOU ARE INCREDIBLY AWESOME..

Hey little soul,Do not be afraid of
things that frighten you..
You are not here to be feared of anything.

Hey little heart,Do not think over on
things that trouble you..
You are not here to be spoilt of overthinking.

Hey little soul, Do not tremble by
the words that fade your dreams..
You are not here to be faded away.

Atlast, O' little heart ! Be who you are.
Because..
You are incredibly awesome only

FEEL THE WIND

by the way you are..

-Mercyba Angel A-

About The Co-Author

-Mercyba Angel A-

Mercyba Angel A ,known for her endless speech is now a budding writer. She always wanted to explore all around. She now took up her pen to express her own feelings through words to explore the minds of others.

TWENTY-NINE
MERRY MIND

Thirsty Thoughts!
Nasty Moods!

Sweet enemies!
Harsh Relatives!

Chat with Unknown!
Mute with Mom!

Digitally Live!
Physically....?!?!

This will tend
Towards the Horizon!

Horizon offers the present to be
HAPPY again!

-Mrs.P.V.RAJLAKSHMI-

About The Co-Author

Mrs.P.V.RAJLAKSHMI

She is currently working as an Assistant Professor. She is passionate about literature from her school days itself. She has published Articles and One-Act plays. The oringin of her interest has been started as a script-writer for her college. Now she has become a social critic through her Research Articles

THIRTY
THE UNLUCKY STAR IN THE SKY

THE UNLUCKY STAR IN THE SKY,

Let us start our story in an unconventional way that is with a question. Have you ever waited in a queue for more than one hour and when it was your turn in the line ,the counter would be closed whether it's a queue for your favourite movie ticket, train ticket or even for a bus ? How would you feel at that moment ? angry,mad etc... What if I tell you that happens as a daily scenario in someone's life ,that some one is me. If your answer to the above question is yes,then we might share the same unlucky DNA which is bestowed on great legends. Just kidding. Why do i say such terrible things ? You might be wondering. I"ll give you some instances. I never really had great desires like other girls ,like buying gold,diamonds even covering or bronze. Things for which i did have a desire for were either pencils or pen or just my favorite breakfast in the morning. Just like the instance i gave above, when it's my turn , the universe some what plays a magic trick and makes it unavailable for me. There is a saying that goes like this: "God's no is not a rejection but rather than a redirection" Wow! so comforting. But i wonder for how long god is going to redirect me. I've had people telling me that "it is just god's test for your patience". All i have to say to them is that i have achieved the epitome of patience that i can even start a monastery with it. The things that I described may sound funny when written in this way but when you have to go through it on a daily basis, you feel like your life is falling apart atleast that's how i feel at times. But still i hope to find that glimmer of light that lies in the darkness.Because hope has always been a game changer through out human history.If it wasn't for the hope that Kalpana Chawla had, she would not have been able to register her name in the history of NASA . Hope gives you wings to fly above the obstacles at hands. So i hope you keep hoping too......

-P.KANIMOZHI-

About The Co-Author

-P.KANIMOZHI-

Kanimozhi is an innovative soul who always brings positivity as a part of her personality.She wishes to bring positivity into everyone's life by her writings.

THIRTY-ONE
BLESSED BY YOU

I can do everything
Start by now never be end
Work with struggle

Don't give up
Don't give in
At any situation

Take time
Gain more
You can
You can it do everything

Successful person
If you want to get success
Change yourself not others

Everyday is New day
But not new sun
Reminder it rise only new but sun is Same

FEEL THE WIND

You is only you
Not others so
Rise like sun
Everyday bring as new thought
It will give success

Baby
Hey my future bby I loved you enter into the world
Tiny toes little finger
So sinsitive skin
I love you so much

Hey my happiness
Your my precious love from god
Mummy eyes dad nose
So cute lips
I love you so much

We are blessed by you
I am took you in my arms
I forgot the hardest thing
You sleep in my hand
My world is you
I love you so much.

-Praisee.M-

About The Co-Author

M.praisee BA

I love to be write poem
My aim is to became a author

THIRTY-TWO
THE POWER OF WOMEN

THE POWER OF WOMEN

We all know that if there are no women in this world, there is no world. Nowadays women in most part of the world are equal to men's power. But in our ancestral times women are only for cooking and maintaining the family. Women are never younger than men that are proved by nowadays women. They are successful and excel in all fields such as from cooking to pilot. If a woman is an educator then the whole family will become an educationist.

According to me, compulsory all women should be encouraged by our society to reach their path of success. This is a very big support to them. But in our society most of the people discouraged them to achieve something. A woman has to face many hardships to make her dreams come true. From the birth of a woman to her death she has to live for others so I wish to change this continuity. Women are the most powerful weapon for our world. Many of them are achieve their goals even in their hardship life. For example we coming to see;i)Mother Teresa *became the first Indian woman to win the Nobel Peace Prize, ii)Kalpana Chawla was the first Indian woman who reached in space, iii) Kiren Bedi become the first woman IPS officer in India and etc., Then In TAMILNADU we see; Velu Natchiyar, Jayalalitha, Nanammal and etc., The only reason for the success of all women is their diligence. The success of a woman depends on her family. A woman's every success after marriage is only because of their husbands so women should be admired by all. Every woman is talented so we have to encourage them and it is our duty to make them succeed. From this part what I am coming to say means don't underestimate women because each and every women has individual talents so let them to achieve something in their life and I wish to say that you help them to reach their goals. The development of women's success has be a very big growth to comparing a days from our ancestral times to the present. Truly I'm saying really I'm very proud to being a Woman. Women are the only person who acts in all vital role which means compare their life between from their birth to till their death, at first she act as a good daughter to her parents, and next she become a respectable woman, then after her marriage she as a true wife to her husband and the next she will be a good mother to her child, then she spend her whole lifetime to her family till her death. So Women have multi talents while comparing to men. So every woman should be proud to being a woman. They should be praised by this whole society, all are should give respect to them and motivate them to achieve success. This is the true power of all women in this world.*

-Sivasankari P-

About The Co-Author

Sivasankari P

She is Sivasankari ,now she is doing M.A English Literature.She have interest in writings.In this anthology she writes about women's power.She likes to write many writings and she is very good in writings.

THIRTY-THREE
INNER SPACE

My Love,
I may not beg for
your long life,
but, if you cut your finger
also, my hear cries.

I may not beg for
your good health,
but, if cold attacks you
also, you will see me upset.

I may not beg for your achievements,
but, if a single backstep
also, makes me sad.

I may not beg for
your increment
but, I pray to keep
as you are...

Instead of all these

FEEL THE WIND

I pray for loads of happiness,
Love, care, affection,
and positive energy
in your life.

2) A friend is a light
when you walk in the dark
a friend is a hopewhen you are in despair
a friend is a joy
when you smile
a friend is a support
a trust, a reflection.

God knows the value of heartr
so HE created love
he knows the value of night
so he created dreams
he knows the value of a friend in my life
so he created you.

3) TRUSTING THE TRUST
How much I loved you
never pondered another thought
you were also like that
nobody was there in your world.

Imagine once
you in my place
me in your place.

forgiving is not great
that's inevitability
but

the pain....

I thought you were Rama
but you are Krishna
I thought I'm Seetha
But you made me Radha.

Seetha felt solace
in fire, because
Nobody is therein the world of Rama.

Though Radha is
Krishna...
she is insecure of Rukmini and Gopikas
and, you know why...

now you tell me
what am I
Seetha....or
Radha...?
-SOWMYA RAJ B.M.-

THIRTY-FOUR

A FRIEND IS A LIGHT

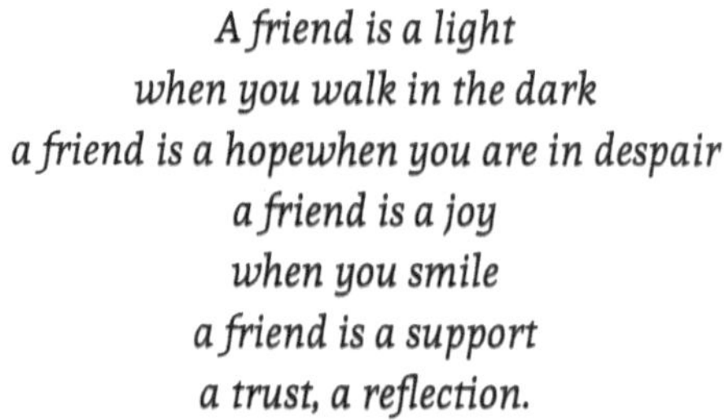

A friend is a light
when you walk in the dark
a friend is a hopewhen you are in despair
a friend is a joy
when you smile
a friend is a support
a trust, a reflection.

God knows the value of heartr
so HE created love
he knows the value of night
so he created dreams
he knows the value of a friend in my life
so he created you.

-SOWMYA RAJ B.M.-

THIRTY-FIVE
TRUSTING THE TRUST

TRUSTING THE TRUST
How much I loved you
never pondered another thought
you were also like that
nobody was there in your world.

Imagine once
you in my place
me in your place.

forgiving is not great
that's inevitability
but
the pain....

I thought you were Rama
but you are Krishna
I thought I'm Seetha
But you made me Radha.

Seetha felt solace
in fire, because
Nobody is therein the world of Rama.

Though Radha is
Krishna...
she is insecure of Rukmini and Gopikas
and, you know why...

now you tell me
what am I
Seetha....or
Radha...?

-SOWMYA RAJ B.M.-

About The Co-Author

Sowmya Rah B.M

Sowmya Rah B.M. works as Assistant Professor in English. she is a versatile poet and has translated many poems from Kannada to English along with writing her own poems in English and Kannada. a young mother with two little twins, she leads life with the thought that everything happens in life for good.

THIRTY-SIX
OPTIMISTIC NYCTOPHILE

Darkness - It is not a negative thing. But everyone think like that. Every darkness has it's own positive side. It's also a phenomenal thing. Don't be afraid of that. It never gives lonely feelings at all. It has a lot of meanings in itself. Positive can't be find in every place or situation. It has to find by a true soul which devotes to God and philosophy. Brightness doesn't give a positive vibes all the time. When everyone become a temporary people in your life, darkness become a only permanent companion to you. Not everyone could understand this. It's a love about lonely pleasure.

Everyone in this world has their own way to live their life. When they get good things, they feel happy and praise the Lord. But when something bad happens, they curse the life and God. That's not a correct way to lead a stable life. People always think about the negativity which is influenced by their surroundings. Likewise, they consider dark as a bad omen. That's totally a superstitious belief. It's a colour of goodness. Black is the only colour that gives meaning to the other colours. When we falling in love with darkness, we could find anything beyond the imagination. That's totally different from other people and thoughts. Optimism comes from the thoughtful mind. It gives us motivation and helps to avoid the pessimistic view of everything.

Night is all about the deep feelings running in our mind as well as heart. Probably everyone does the same thing in their life. They express various feelings in that time. Like, crying, dreaming, imagining, motivating and so on. We don't feel these things in the day time. Because it's uncomfortable to act as a weirdo. Overthinking is a cause of our illness, instead of that we can keep a deep thinking. It helps to heal ourselves. Every problem has it's own solution...we should find that without falling down. Our pillows act as a best friend in that hard times. So being an "OPTIMSTIC NYCTOPHILE" is a precious thing for our mental health.

"The one who loves the DARKNESS, never hates the BRIGHTNESS...but

The one who loves the BRIGHTNESS can easily hates the DARKNESS"

*- **Sri***

THIRTY-SEVEN
ILLUSIONED LIFE

Illusion...where we can find ourselves. Everyone is struggle with their life. They want to earn money and everything. But i think that these kind of things give us a temporary happiness. When we decided to think differently, life give us a chance to escape from the struggled life. That's none other than LIVING IN AN IMAGINATION WORLD. We don't have to fight for anything there. We can live several lives in that illusioned life. There we can get enough happiness and not to worry much about anything. There is no one to hurt us. We should play our role perfectly and have fun. That is possible when we start to read GOOD BOOKS by ourselves without any regret or compulsion. When we start to learn the inner feelings through books, we don't have to struggle with the outer world or people.

We share our feelings to ourselves. We don't have to expect anyone to hear or help us. We could fetch support by our own confidence. It lead us to have a good and proper living with peacefulness. The outer world is nothing in front of the feeling where we could get a lot of experience and pleasure. This lead us to face all the problems with smile and hope on getting success. Everyone thinks that illusion is all about day dreaming. That's totally wrong. They conclude this beautiful word with these simple words. But in reality...Illusion is an indescribable word. It gives meaning to those who are ready to hear it's voice. Not everyone can live in this world. It costs very muck...such as patience, peace and smile. We must have tolerance to enter into this world. Books are always an underrated things. We should cling on that. When no one is ready to hear our thoughts and feelings, they give us a different kind of feeling. That is...we don't have to share our thoughts or feelings to others and to the world. We can keep ourselves as a priority and make good communication to our own conscience. Then we can feel our importance.

People come into our life and give us a good and bad memories. But when we listen to books, they only give us good memories and lessons. On that moment, we can realize the original world and what actually life is...

It's all about to listen ourselves, make decision by ourselves, love ourselves, give priority to ourselves. When we are really happy, we will definitely make others happy without any doubt. Create your own illusion world and live there peacefully...that brings you to get a lot of EUPHORIA.

"Live in your own NATION...That's your IMAGINATION"

- Sri

THIRTY-EIGHT
SCARE

What scares you the most? I replied without any hesitation...That's PEOPLE. Yes, I scared to people very much. Because they judge us, criticise us, mock us and make us to feel embarrassed. They always find faults in others. But not in themselves. Everyone make mistake at some point. People can judge easily without knowing anything fully. No matter what we have done good things for all the time. When we made something bad unintentionally, they will started to criticise us. It's not our fault but everything start from us. Actually, we are not blaming the society or people, they only made us to do so. When we try to ignore these things, they will start to fabricate the unnecessary stuffs. In that situation..we don't have to react whether it is good or bad and also there is no need to mingle with others or to the society. When we make decisions or do something important, we always afraid of people. Like... How will they react?...What is the consequences of our action?. Above all, everyone in this world might afraid of people. Their impact plays an important role in our life.

Our actions, behaviours, mannerism...all of these are calculated by the people. They want us to be perfect without any flaws. The biggest fault in people is that they compare everything by their own. They gossip everything without any regret. We are really try to understand them, but they don't give a chance to us. The real fact is...no one in this world can understand everything or everyone to the fullest. We don't have that power. When we try to understand someone, it all goes wrong. We must understand the reality than people. Listen to music and nature than you listen to people. That can help you to understand the difference between expectations and reality. We should give up our expectations over reality. Likewise, don't expect people to understand our point of view.

And finally... Be you, no matter what. Don't care about other people for judging you. Give yourself happiness. They do whatever they want, stay away from the negative people. Do your thing with good vibes.

Don't be scared of anything but people. Even negative has it's own little positive. Likewise, people also make us to do the right things.

"Not every SCARE is bad... Some scare give us the REASON TO MOVE ON".

- Sri

About The Co-Author

-Sri-

"Things happens for a reason" is the motto of her life. She takes everything positive as possible as she can. She believes in fate and loves to write.

THIRTY-NINE
OPEN LETTER TO MY MIND

It is only an imagination. The following things which i could imagine what i feel when i feel the wind. It did not have an end i can alternate what i will think about it.

It's a breeze spread my hair frizzy when i am in the top of my house's empty floor. Wind signalizes what i got in the past. Both good and bad moments and memorizes my happiness and sorrow. In my childhood days, when i feel the wind it explains how i enjoyed my funny past days in and how i will enjoy my life. Like when i feel the wind i had one main thing that is i had swang a little swing in a mango tree. Then i had flew a kite. Wind also blow evrything in my mind.

When i feel the wind, it describes about travel when i had some good music and the better long journey and the companion of my favourite persons, friends, relatives or my solumate. When i feel the wind my bind blowing to paly a music and want to notify the lyrics of the song minutely. Music heals everything. Do you know how music diverts my mind? It is a boon for me to avoid overthinking. Because mind wants to change the music whatever our mindset may be.

When i feel the wind i want to think about my best ones. They may be my parents, friends, bffs, besties and the main person that is may be my soulmate. Soulmate is the only one who will enjoy, criticise and make my life so happy and smileful and anger with me. He will made my life so beautiful and pleasant. Soulmate is the person who can made all those things with me in my life more surprisingly, beautifully and make the pleasure and sweetness to my mind.

When i feel the wind i want to hd my soulmate's hand and tell something about. It may be good or bad. Good things may be happened later. But those can be made my life so beautiful.

To the person, where i wants to go and what i wants to live with him is also go through in my dreams but it will happened in future. So, that when i feel the wind i explore something about soulmate.

When i married my man, at that time, i will feel the wind means it give more things to imagine where we will go? and where we will come? with my soulmate. These are making a priceless memories.

When i feel the wind i want to think about something which make my mind so upset and the person who make me upset. But at the same tme will will think about what are the stupid things we would make it for them. These are remembering memories when i feel the wind.

When i feel the wind at the sea, i want to play with sea water and i want to make a fun with sand and make my own sand castles eating streetfoods. It gives more and more pleasure to all.

People can get their feelings when they feel the wind and also remembered memories which they had already get.

When i feel the wind after getting a child may be i will think about how can i secure my childrens life? and what i have to done for them?

Take your own imagination with my words. We are in a bright and blossoming place. The flowers were glooming beautifukky. Flowers are so beautiful and they shine as charming as stars. It's a bliss when we see this scenerio with the help of wind. Thats it.

When i feel ill, the wind boost up and cheer up my helath to be good and better.

When i feel the wind it takes more pleasant and beautiful journey ahead.

When i feel the wind, my mind can blow all thoughts. Sometimes the wind can be irritate for me. But always companion is wind that makes my life so fresh, pure, blissful and confidence.

Somepeople can say temple have a pure wind. When i feel the wind from the temple my mind will be fresh as pure as a blossoming flowers.

When i feel the wind after my child getting married i feel complete and i feel it's enough to work for our childrens. Lets take a break and want to live a stressless life. Then i want to live a retirement life as casual as ripe life. I want to enjoy my remaining days with my soulmate then me and my man want to play with my grand childrens.

When i feel the wind, it takes out pathological conditions and situations. When i am in a sluggish mind, it bring full energy to my mind to stand up and do some activities.

If you want a pithy comment by me means wind is the pure, powerful feelings and emotions. So i can enjoy my life. So, be happy and live with your own way as a normal human being don't overthinking about stupid things.

I want to live a pleasure and satisfaction usually, but sometimes you kept me to overthink and you pull me into depressed thoughts. I kindly requested you to give me some empty mind only with happiness and for my life without

overthinking.
Many times, you give a pageantary scemes that is some good
and bad things.
These are some simple things which i could imagine when i feel
the wind. I dont want to be panic. So, i want to be a proficient
person in my life.

-Sujanasri jambukeswaran-

About The Co-Author

Sujanasri jambukeswaran

Sujanasri jambukeswaran who is pursuing her B.A English Literature degree. She want to read a tragedic and romatic novels ahead. "Don't let others give an oppurtunity fo your life, you can construct your own life". She is one of the co-author in an anthology "Affection". "Achievements can be noticed with how we worked for that". Mail id: sujanasrij7555@gmail.com

FORTY

முடிவற்ற பயணம் ..

மனதின் இறுக்கத்தை கரைக்கவே நீ வந்தாயோ...
ஒரே ஒரு அணைப்பில் உலகமே நீயென மாறியது மனம்...
மழையோடு ஒரு பயணம் தொடர்ந்தேன்
கால்களெல்லாம் நனைந்தபடி என்னைக் கொஞ்சிட
இன்னொரு முறை என நான் அதை கெஞ்சிட...
காதல் வயப்பட்டோம் நானும் மழையையும்...
அமைதியாய் ஒரு சலசல
மழையின் சத்தம் மட்டும் காதில் இசையாய் கேட்டிட...
இலைகள் மேல் விழுந்த மழைத்துளி
என் மீது தெறிக்க இன்னும் களசிப் போனேன் நான்..
காற்றோடு காற்றாய் ஆடிய மரக்கிளைகள்
மழையோடு என் மனமும் கொட்டித் தீர்த்து விட...
இந்த மழையின் கொஞ்சலும்
என் கெஞ்சலும் இன்னும் தொடர வேண்டும்
முடிவற்ற பயணமாய்...
-கள்ளியின் கிறுக்கல்-

FORTY-ONE

இரகசிய காதல் கணினியோடு

❤

ஆரம்பத்தில் அறமை நிழுவதும் நிறைந்த நீ
இன்று என்னுள் நிறைந்த காதல் கொண்டாய் கைக்குள்..
உலகையே உன்னுள் வைத்திருக்கும் உனக்கு
என் மனம் கொண்ட இரகசியம் புரியவில்லையா?
வாழ்வில் அதிக நேரம் செலவிட்டனே உன்னோடு
இயந்திரமான உனக்குள் காதல் இல்லை என்று உணராமல் ...
நான் தனிமையில் தவித்த போதெல்லாம்
என் மனம் தடேய துணை நீயே...
பல நாள் சந்தேகம் எனக்கு, இந்த காதல்
உன் மேலோ..?! உனக்கும் இருக்கிறாள் என் காதல் என்பதாலா..?!
பல மணிநேரே ஒத்திகை பார்த்தேன் உரையாடலுக்காக
ஒரு நொடியில் ஒரு பொத்தானைக் கொண்டு அழித்து
விட்டாயே..!!

FORTY-TWO

என் அறையோடு நான்

தூசு தட்டி பார்க்க வேண்டியதாய் இருந்தது
என்றோ ஒரு நாள் திறந்த என் அறையை...!
ஜன்னல்களெல்லாம் என்னை விடுதலை செய்
என்றே கூச்சலிட்டு நின்றது...!
உள்ளே வந்ததும் வராததுமாய்
என் அறைக்கு வெளிச்சம் கொடுக்கவே தோன்றியது...!
ஜன்னலை திறந்தபடி நூல்களிடம் சென்றது
அவை நலம் விசாரித்து பக்கங்களை திருப்பின காற்றோடு...!
பல நினைவுகள் எனக்குள் வந்து போக
அறையே அமைதியாய் மாறிப் போனது...!
வெளியில் உலகமே மாறிப்போய் இருந்த நிலையில்
அறை மட்டும் அதே நினைவுகளுடன் மனம் மாற்றிக் கொள்ள
இயலா நான் ...!

FORTY-THREE
கவிஞன் நான்

———♡———

தனி உலகினில் நானும் என்
பனோவாவும்-! மீழ்வாேமா? கேள்வியுடன் ...
கவலையிலமும் இரசிக்கிறேன் - காதல்
பித்து நான் கசக்கிய காகிதத்தின் மேல்!
பித்தனா ? சித்தனா? விந்தையாய் என்
கற்பனை கனவுகள் கலயை மறுத்து ...
நிராகரிப்புகள் ஆயிரம் - நித்தம்
என் நிஜம் புரியாத உயிரினங்களால் !
வித்தியாச விளக்கவுரைகள் பல
எனக்கும் என் நிழலுக்கும் ...!
என் மீது கோபம் எனக்கே
ஏன் மீழ வேண்டும் - சக மனிதனாய் அவதியுறவா?
நான் வித்தியாசத்தின் உச்சம் - உலகை
உலகாய் பார்க்கும் அவர்கள் எங்கே!
இரசனையின் மொத்த உருவமாய் பார்க்கும் நான் எங்கே ...
வார்த்தைகளை, உயிரை கொடுத்து தடேுகிறேன்
எவ்வாறு புரிய வைப்பேன் என் மனதின் நிலயை ...
பனோவவாேடு தான் என் வாழ்க்கை என்று நான்
கல்லறை செல்லவும் தயார்...
கடசி மூச்சு வரை பனோவவாேடு என்றால்

பயணம் தொடரட்டும் இல்லையேல்,
முடித்துக்கொள்வேன் மழையோடு சேர்த்து என்
பயணத்தையும் ..

FORTY-FOUR

நீயில்லா நேரம்

நாள் முழுவதும் உன் ஸ்பரிசம் ஒன்றே
நான் ஏங்கும் மௌச்சாக இருக்கும்..!
என் மழலையான நேரங்களோடு நீயும்
குழந்தையாய் மாறிப்போனாய் அப்பா..!
முதல்முறை உன்னை விட்டு தூரம் போகும் நான்
மனம் கலங்கிய சிரிப்புடன்..!
இந்த சமூகத்தைக் கண்டு நான் அஞ்சும் போது
சட்டையினுள் ஒலித்துக் கொண்டு காத்தாய்..!
முழுமையாய் வளர்ந்த மரத்தை பிடுங்கி
வேறோடு வேறு இடம் கொண்டு செல்ல துணிகிறார்கள்..!
எப்படி வளர்ந்து செழிக்க போகிறதோ?
பாழாய் போன இந்த சமூகத்தின் முந்நிலையில்..!
உணர்வுகளெல்லாம் உடைந்து போய் நிற்கிறேன்
நானும் மகன் அல்லாமல் மகளாய் பிறந்த இவள் ...

FORTY-FIVE

இரவோடு பயணம்

கவலைகள் பின் தொடர்ந்து கொண்டே இருக்க
விரல் அணைப்போடு ஒரு பயணம் போதும்...!
இரவின் பிடியில் இப்படியே சிறுதூரம்
இனி ஏதும் தடேயுமா? இந்த இதயம்...!
ஒருவரும் இல்லா இருட்டு சாலை
காய்ந்த இலைகளின் சத்தம் ஒன்றே பாதங்களுக்கு அடியில்...!
கண் காணும் தூரம் வரை
இந்த இரு இதயங்களின் சத்தம் மட்டுமே...!
என்றும் அழிக்க முடியாத நினைவாய் மாறியது
மனதின் விருப்பமான நபருடன் செலவிட்ட தருணங்கள்..!
நிகழும் தினம் என்று நினைத்த நிமிடங்கள் யாவும்
இன்று நினைவுகளாய் மாறிப்போக...!
கண்ணீர் துடைக்க கரங்கள் தடேயும்
மனநிலையையோ நமக்கு...!
கைகள் நீட்டிடாமல் போனால் என்ன
என்றோ கூறிச் சென்ற வார்த்தைகள் நம்மோடு...
என்றும் இனிமையான பயணம்
நம் தனிமையின் விரல்களை பிடித்தபடியே...!
தீர்ந்து போகாத பாதையில் தனிமையில் இனிமை...!

FEEL THE WIND

-Narmadha.S -

About The Co-Author

-Narmadha. S-

She's Narmadha. Her birth place is Erode District. She completed her bachelor of English Literature. Her dream and passion is to become a famous writer. She started her writing due to her stress then she realised some happiness and peace of mind in writing. That made her pen nib so strong.

FORTY-SIX

எனது பார்வையில் இயற்கை

விண்ணிலிருந்து வரும்
மழைத்துளிகள் ஒவ்வொன்றும்...
சொல்கிறது நான் இயற்கையின் அழகை
பார்க்க துடிக்கிறேன் என்றது...
அத்துளிகள் இயற்கையின் அழகு
பார்த்து வர்ணிக்க வார்த்தை இல்லை என்றது...
மலையிலிருந்து வரும் நீரோடை
போல என் மனமும்...
உனது அலைகளின் நிலை கண்டு
என் மனமும் கரைகிறது...
மரங்கள் கூறியது காற்றுக்கு நன்றி
காற்று வீசி என்னை மேலும்
அழகாக்கியதற்கு என்று தலையசைத்தது...

-சௌமியா.அ

FORTY-SEVEN
மழை

கரு௫கேங்கள் சூழ்ந்த௫ சூரியனின்
ஒளியை மறைத்த௫...
நீரோடையின் நீராவியைக்
கடன் வாங்கி...
அனைத்த௫ உலகமு௫ம் இரு௫ள் சூழ்ந்தபடி
மக்களின் பார்வையை மேல்வாங்கி...
பலத்த காற்று௫டன் ஓசையு௫டன் கூடிய
மு௫ழக்கத்த௫டன்...
அனைத்த௫ மலைகளின் அழகு௫ம்
வெளிப்பட...
பறவைகள் கூடு௫களில் தங்கிட
நீரோடைகள் மழையைப் பார்த்த௫ பயந்த௫...
பெரிய அலைகளு௫டன் கூடிய ஒரு௫
சத்தத்தை எழு௫ப்பி...
நீ என்னு௫டன் வந்தால் கூட்டிச் செல்வேன் உன்னை
என்னு௫டைய பு௫திய உலகத்திற்கு௫...
மழையு௫ம் சொன்னத௫ நான் வரு௫வதால்
தான் நீயு௫ம் செல்கிறாய் அங்கே என்றத௫...

-சௌமியா.அ

FORTY-EIGHT

நிலா

இரவில் விண்ணைக்க அழகை
சேர்ப்பத நிலவை...
உனத அழகைக் கண்ட வியப்பதால்
வர வதால் கனவ...
பறவைகள் சொன்னத
உன் அழகை இரசிக்க நேரேமில்லையென்ற...
நிலா கூறியத,உன் அழகை
இரசிக்க இன்ன ம் வெளிச்சம் வேண்ட மென்றத...
கண்ணன் கர இமகைகள்
உனத ஆடை...
உன் அழக கண்ட
பொங்கி எழ ந்தத நீரோடை...
வெள்ளை முத்த போல்
உனத வெளிச்சம்...
உன் அழக கண்ட
க யில் பாடியத பாட்ட...

-சௌமியா.அ

FORTY-NINE

சூரியன்

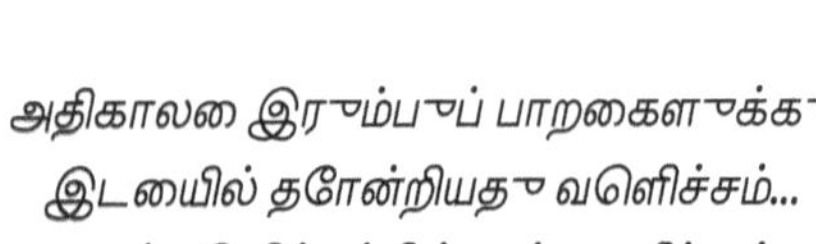

அதிகாலை இரும்பப் பாறைகளுக்கு
இடையில் தோன்றியது வெளிச்சம்...
அவ்வெளிச்சத்தில் உள்ள கதிர்கள்
பூமியில் பட்ட அசுத்தம் அழிந்தது...
இரும்பப் பாறைகளுக்கு இடையில்
எட்டிப் பார்த்தது சூரியன்...
மரங்களெல்லாம் அவசர படவே
வேகமாய் வெளியே வந்தது சூரியன்...

-சௌமியா.அ

FIFTY

ஓவியம்

நான் பார்க்காத உலகை
உன்னூள் பார்க்க வரைந்தேன் ...
என்னிலடங்காத வண்ணங்கள்
உன்னூள் அடக்கினாய்...
பூதூ உலகம் படைத்தாய் என்னூள்
வண்ணங்களாய் அழியாமல்
கரூமையான இருூட்டூ கூட
வண்ணமயமாய்...
உலகை படைப்பேன்
பூதூவிதமாய்
என் எண்ணங்களை வண்ணமாக
மாற்றியபடி...

-சௌமியா.அ

About The Co-Author

FIFTY-ONE
நிலாப் பாட்டி

பின் இரவு ஒன்பது மணி என்பதை கோயில் மணியின் ஒசையில் அறிந்து பள்ளி வீட்டு வேலைகளை எல்லாம் முடித்துவிட்டு தயிர்ச்சட்டி போல் இருக்கும் நிலாவைக்காண வீட்டு முற்றத்திற்கு போனேனே எதைக்கேட்டாலும் ஆராயும் ஐந்து வயது சிறுமி ஆகிய நான். நேற்று தாத்தா சொன்னது உண்மையையோ என ஆராயவே போனேனே. நேற்று நான் என் தாத்தாவிடம் சென்று எங்கே எனது பாட்டி? நான் பள்ளி சென்று வரும் போது எனக்குப்டி அனைத்து வரவேற்பா என் கதைகளை எல்லாம் ஆசையாக கேட்பா எனக்கும் நல்ல கதைகள் எல்லாம் சொல்லுவா. எப்போதும் குனிந்தபடியே நடக்கும் பாட்டி எனக்கு தான் நிமிர்ந்து நடந்து காட்டுறன் என்று சொன்னவா. முதுகு நோ என்று ஆஸ்பத்திரி போன பாட்டி ஏன் இன்னும் திரும்பி வரவில்லை. இப்ப அவ நிமிர்ந்து நடப்பாவா? ஏன் இன்னும் என்னைப்பார்க்க வரவில்லை. என் நண்பர்கள் அனைவரும் அவர்கள் பாட்டியிடம் சென்றுதான் கதை கேட்பார்கள் நானும் என்பாட்டியிடம் கதை கேட்க வேண்டும். எப்பதான் பாட்டி வருவா எங்க இருக்கிறா? என்று கேட்டேனே. என்கேள்விக்கெல்லாம் பதில் சொல்லாமல் தாத்தா

நிலாவைப்பார்த்வாறே நின்றார். 'ஏன் தாத்தா நிலாவைப்பார்த்துக்கொண்டே நிற்கிறீங்க? பாட்டி என்ன நிலாவிலயோ இருக்கிறா' இது நான். தாத்தா அமைதியாக 'என்ன சொல்லம் சொன்னீங்க ஆமா பாட்டி நிலவிலா தானம்மா இருக்கிறா அது தான் பார்க்கிறேன்' என்றார். என்ன தாத்தா எங்க நானும் பார்க்கிறன் என்று நான் கேட்ட போது கொடிய கருமேகேங்கள் நிலாவை மறைத்து விட்டது. என்ன தாத்தா இந்த மேகேங்கள் நிலாவை மறைச்சிடுச்சே பாட்டியை இந்த மேகேங்களா கொண்டு போச்ச என்று கேட்டேன்.

"ஓ! பாட்டி மலேே ஒன்னுமயெில்ல ஏன் குனிஞ்சு குனிஞ்சு நடக்கிறீங்க. நல்லா நிமிந்து நடவுங்க பாட்டி" என்று நான்தானே பாட்டிக்கு அடிக்கடி கூறினேன். நான் பள்ளியால வரேக்க தான் நிமிந்து நடக்கிறன் என்று பாட்டி சொன்னவாதானே. "ஓ!! என்ர சொல்லக்கேட்ட பாட்டி நிமிந்து நடக்கேக்க மேகேத்தில முட்டிருச்சோ. அது தான் மேகேத்துக்கு கோபம் வந்து பாட்டியை மலேே குட்டிக்கொண்டு நிலாவில விட்டிருச்சா. சொல்லுங்க தாத்தா சொல்லுங்க" என்று நான் கேட்டேன்.

தாத்தாவும் அமைதியாக "ஆமா கண்ணு" என்று சொன்னார். "இந்த மேகேங்கள் ஒருக்கா கீழ வந்தால் நானும் அதில ஏறி பாட்டியிட்ட போகலாம் தான தாத்தா?" என்று கேட்க தாத்தா கண்கள் கலங்கியவாறே என்னைப் பார்த்தார். "ஏன் தாத்தா இந்த மேகேங்கள் தான் ஒரே நிலாவைச்சுற்றி படைவீரர்கள் மாறி ரோந்து போகுதே எப்ப இது கீழே வரும். பாட்டி முன்பு வடையைல்லாம் சுட்டுத்தருவா எவ்வளவு ருசி. தாத்தா பாட்டி அங்க என்ன தான் செய்யிறா சொல்லுங்க தாத்தா" என்று கேட்டேன். சோகமாக விருந்த தாத்தா இப்போது தான், " ஆமா குட்டி அவ வடை தான் சுடுறா செல்லத்திற்கு" என்றார். கரு மேகேங்களிலிருந்து வெண்ணிலா எப்போது

தெரியும்.பாட்டியை எப்போது காணலாம் என்று காத்திருந்து தாத்தாவின் மடியில் அயர்ந்து தூங்கி விட்டேனே.

இப்போது கூட நிலவிலிருக்கும் பாட்டியை பார்க்த்தான் வீட்டு முற்றத்திற்கு வந்தேனே. கன்றுக்குட்டியிடம் தாய்ப்பசு செல்வதைப் போல் என் மூன்று வயது தங்கையும் என் பின்னாலே வந்தாள். "ஏன் அக்கா நிலாவைப் பார்க்கிறாய்?" என்று என்னைக் கேட்க நானும் பாட்டியைப்பற்றி அவளிடம் சொன்னேன். பிறகு இருவரும் நிலவை உற்றுப் பார்க்க விரைந்தோம். நாம் பாட்டியின் காண்பதற்கு முன்னரே என் இரு அண்ணன்களும் சதுரங்கம் விளையாட எம்மை அழைத்துவிட்டனர். பாட்டியை பார்க்க வேண்டும் என்ற ஏக்கம் எனக்குள் இருந்தது. ஆனால் அண்ணன் அழைத்தால் விளையாட சென்று விட்டோம். என் அப்பாவின் தோள்களை ஆசனம் போல் நினைத்து ஏறி உட்கார்ந்து கொண்டேன். பஞ்சை தெரிக்கும் போது எந்த உணர்ச்சியும் இல்லாத போல் என் தந்தையும் நான் ஏறியதே தெரியாமல் இருந்தார். என் இரண்டாவது அண்ணனும் அப்பாவும் பதற்றமாக சதுரங்கத்தை விளையாடினார். நான் பிறந்த பொழுதில் இருந்தே சதுரங்க விளையாட்டு என்றாள் எங்கள் வீட்டில் களொள்ளைப்பிரியம். வீட்டில் அனைவரும் சதுரங்கம் விளையாடுவோம் என்ன விந்தை என்றால் அனைவரும் என் மூன்று வயதான கடைக்குட்டியிடம் தோற்று விடுவோம். அவள் நன்றாக சதுரங்கம் விளையாடுவாள் நன்கு பயிற்சி பெற்ற தந்தை கூட இலகுவாக தோற்றுவிடுவார். யானைக்கும் எறும்பைக்கண்டால் பயம் போல் எமக்கும் சதுரங்க விளையாட்டில் தங்கையுடன் விளையாடுவது என்றாள் பயம் இப்படியாக கூடும்பமே ஒன்றாக சதுரங்க விளையாட்டு விளையாடும் போது எனக்கு மட்டும் மனம் முழுவதும் நிலாவே இருந்தது. நேரம் இரவு பத்து மணி

ஆகிவிட்டது சதுரங்க விளையாட்டை முடித்துவிட்ட அனைவரும் இரவு உணவை உண்ண விரைந்தோம். அன்று இரவு எனது அம்மா தோசையை சுட்டார் இராக்கம் ஆசையையும் கூட்டி விட்டார். நிலாவைப்போல் தோசையும் வட்டமாக அழகாக இருந்தது. அப்போது என் தாத்தா 'நிலாவை பார்த்தீங்களா குட்டி என்று பாசமாகவே கேட்டார். இல்லை என்று வாடியமுகத்துடன் சொன்னேன். 'சரி நாளை பார்க்கலாம்' என்று பிஞ்சு மனதை தேற்றினார். அனைவரும் தூங்கச்சென்றோம். பிறப்பதற்கு முன் தாயின் வயிற்றில் எவ்வாறு சுருண்டு உள்ளே இருப்பேமோ அதைப்போல் நானும் என் தாயின் வயிற்றுப்பகுதக்குள் சுருண்டு படுத்துக்கொண்டேன் நாளை ஞாயிற்றுக்கிழமை அனைவருக்கும் விடுமுறை அதனாலயே தாமதமாக தூங்கினோம். கதைகூட இன்று நான் கேக்கவில்லை தெரியுமா? ஏன் என்றால் ஒரு கதை கேட்டாள் அதை ஆராய்ந்து விட்டுத்தான் அடுத்த கதை கேடக வேண்டும் என்று ஒரு குணம் என்னுள். தாமதமாக தூங்கியும் தூக்கம் வரவில்லை ஏன் என்றால் நிலவை பார்க்க வேண்டும் என்ற ஏக்கம். ஆனால் என் தங்கையோ அப்பாவின் நெஞ்சை மெத்தை பேோல் வைத்து தூங்கியும் விட்டாள். அவளுக்கு நிலாவை பார்க்கவேண்டும் எண்ணமே இல்லை போல. ஆனால் என்னால் தூங்க முடியவில்லை. அம்மாவின் வயிற்றுக்குள் சுருண்டு சுருண்டு பார்த்தேன். நள்ளிரவும் ஆகிவிட்டது. தனியாக வெளியே போய் நிலாவை பார்க்க பயம். ஏனென்றால் இரவில் இருட்டாகவிருக்கும் அல்லாவா. நாளை பார்க்கலாம் என்று மனதை நானே தேற்றிக்கொண்டு தூங்கினேன். மனதில் இருப்பதே கனவில் வரும் என்ற உண்மையையும் அன்றே புரிந்து கொண்டேன். ஏனென்றால் எனக்கு வந்த கனவு அப்படி. நானும் தங்கையும் நிலாப்பாட்டி வீட்டிற்கு

சென்றோம். சென்று கதவை தட்டிய போது பாட்டி 'வாறேன் வாறேன்' என ஓசை எழுப்பினார். கதவை திறந்தால் உண்மையியலேயே எங்கள் பாட்டி வடை தான் சுட்டார். எமக்கும் அந்த வடையை தந்து உண்ணும்படி சொன்னார். நன்றாக கனவு சென்று கொண்டிருக்கும் பொழுது கனவிலிருந்த என்னை என் தங்கை "அக்கா எழும்பு எழும்பு" என்று என்னை எழுப்பினார். கனவோ கலைந்தது. காலை எழும்பி நேரத்தை பார்த்தால் நேரம் பத்து மணி தங்கையோ என்னை விட்டு விட்டு தாத்தாவோடு குளித்து விட்டாள். தாத்தாமலே அறியாப்பருவத்தில் கோபம் கொண்ட நான் கோபத்தை வெளிப்படுத்த தெரியாது அழுதேன். தாத்தா 'சரி சரி குட்டிக்கு நான் குளிக்க வாத்து விடுறேன்' என்றார். அழுகை நின்றது. அழகாக குளித்து விட்டு கொண்டை போட முடியாத என் தலைமுடியில் நானே கொண்டை போட்டு ஒளவையார் போல் திருநீறை நெற்றியில் பூசிவிட்டு வந்தேன். என் பத்து வயது அண்ணா வட்டமாக தன் நெற்றியில் சந்தனப்பொட்டு வைத்திருந்தார். சந்தனப்பொட்டை பார்த்த எனக்கோ மறுபடியும் நிலாவே ஞாபகம் வந்தது. இம்முறை நிலாப்பாட்டி மட்டுமன்றி அந்தக் கனவும் ஞாபகம் வந்தது. எனக்கு வந்த கனவை மிக சந்தோசமாக தாத்தா, அண்ணன்மார்கள், கடைக்குட்டி, அப்பா, அம்மா என அனைவருக்கும் கூறினேன். ஒருவழியாக அந்த நாளின் பகல் பொழுதை கழிக்க நானும் தங்கையும் யோசித்து நிலாப்பாட்டியை வரவைதற்காக ஆயத்தமானோம். நான் செய்யும் அனைத்தையும் கண்ணாடி செய்வது போல் என் தங்கையும் என்னைப்போலவே எல்லாவற்றையும் செய்வாள். தற்போது சித்திரம் கூட அப்படித்தான். காந்தள் பூப்போன்ற மென்மையான விரல்களினால் அழகான வட்டமொன்றை போட்டோம். அதற்கு நிலா என்று பெயர் வைத்து அதற்குள்

வடை சுடுவதற்கு தேவையான பாத்திரம், கரண்டி என்பற்றை எல்லாம் வைத்து விட்டோம். ஆனால் பாட்டியை வரைய மறந்து விட்டோம். என் தங்கைதான் 'அக்கா எங்கே நிலாப்பாட்டி?' என்று வினாவினாள். அவள் கூறிய அடுத்த நிமிடமே பாட்டியை வரைய ஆரம்பித்தேன். வரைந்தும் முடித்தேன். வீட்டின் சுவரில் அம்மா அவித்த சோறை பசைபோல் ஒட்டி வரைந்த சித்திரத்தையும் அதில் ஒட்டிக்கொண்டோம். சிறுவர்கள் இருக்கும் வீடு எப்படியோ அது போல் எங்கள் வீட்டுச் சுவரிலும் சித்திரங்களே இருந்தன. பொழுதும் கழிந்தது. தேநீருடன் வடையைச் சாப்பிட்டுக்கொண்டு நிலாவிற்காக காத்துக்கிடந்தேன். நிலாவும் வந்தது. உற்றுக்கவனித்தேன். என்னவொரு வியப்பு! பாட்டி வடை சுடுவது தெரிந்தது. தள்ளிக்குதித்து தாத்தாவிடம் சென்று "கண்டு விட்டேன், நான் பாட்டியை கண்டு விட்டேன்" என கத்திச்சொல்லிக்கொண்டே அடுத்த கதையைக்கேட்க காத்திருந்தேன். புதிய கதை தாத்தா கூறினாலும் மனம் முழுவதும் நிலாப்பாட்டியே இருந்தாள். அன்றிரவு நிம்மதியாக தூங்கி விட்டு பாலர் பாடசாலைக்குச் சென்று என் நண்பர்கள், ஆசிரியர்கள் அனைவரிடத்தும் அந்தக் கதையை சொன்னேன். அனைவரும் தாங்களும் சென்று பார்ப்பதாக கூறினர். முழுமதி நாளில் பாட்டியை வடிவாக பார்க்கலாம். நான் அதற்காகா காத்திருக்கிறேன்...

-வைஷ்ணவி சிவாஸ்கரன்
இலங்கை-